DR BETH LEIGH

Must you marry?

First edition

This book was professionally typeset on Reedsy
Find out more at reedsy.com

Dedicated to my sweet parents Mr and Mrs Benjamin and to my second parents Mr and Mrs Vincent.

Contents

Foreword

Marriage is not a do or die affair. Being married doesn't make you the best and being unmarried doesn't make you the worst either,you can be married and still not do well and you can be unmarried and still do well and Excel,it all depends on you if you can t endure all in marriage or if you cant give in all to get that perfect marriage,then marriage isn't for you,but if you can you can go ahead but note this ,marriage comes with hiccups,ups and downs.

Acknowledgement

I acknowledge God for making my write up a possible one.

One

MEANING OF MARRIAGE

Marriage means many different things, to many different people. It can be difficult to find a universally applicable, true meaning of what marriage is. There are so many differing viewpoints on this subject and people often disagree about what marriage means to them.

For example, the Oxford Dictionary definition of marriage is, “The legally or formally recognized union of two people as partners in a personal relationship.” However, in a biblical sense marriage is often defined as, “A man shall leave his father and mother… and hold fast his wife… they shall become one flesh.”

Christians often view marriage as a Holy Covenant before God. It seems that the understanding that two people become one unit, pledging their love for each other, is the general consensus across most believers.

It could therefore be argued that most people would buy into the fact that marriage is the sharing of two lives, bonding their spirits, bodies and souls in union. This article will explore five different definitions of what a marriage could mean, in the endeavor to move towards a more cohesive definition of marriage.

1_Marriage means to be in agreement.

In the modern world it is usually acknowledged that in order to enter the bonds of Holy Matrimony, both parties involved must be in agreement. Surely, in order to go on a life-long journey together, both people must have agreed to do so.

In the past, or currently in some belief systems, this agreement was often made by the family members of the happy couple. However, nowadays it is generally agreed that the two people who are to become married, decide this for themselves.

This normally follows the structure of one member of the couple asking the question, "Will you marry me?" If an answer is given in the affirmative, planning the marriage (and the wedding) will go ahead.

Once two people have decided that marriage is for them, they have to decide upon what their true meaning of marriage is. Often the couple will discuss the topic of what legal marriage contract they will use. Other important agreements involve whether to have children, if so, what faith to raise the children and what marriage means to them as a couple.

2_Marriage should mean letting go of selfishness.

It has been discussed that marriage is the joining of two people, therefore it goes without saying that there will need to be some level of compromise. Once you get married there is no more 'I', it's all about 'we'. As a single person you may have been able to do whatever you fancied, to come and go as you pleased, but once you are married, there is another person you need to take into consideration. You need to think about what makes them happy and use this when you are making plans.

The best marriages are often those where both partners are wholly committed to making their other half happy. In a marriage, often this is a priority and by letting go of selfishness and prioritizing your partner you can truly get the best out of a marriage.

2b_Marriage means two become one.

Sticking with the theme of two people becoming one, marriage means blending two lives into one. The most obvious thing you may think of is the physical, sexual intimacy. This can create a profound bond between two people, when the marriage is consummated. Having a healthy sexual relationship is a key aspect of a good marriage. This means different things to different people and is something you should probably discuss with your partner before the wedding bells ring.

The philosophy behind two people becoming one extends far beyond the physical. It should also touch the emotional, spiritual and psychological parts of your relationship. This does not mean that you need to lose your identity, on the contrary you will gain more of an identity, changing and complementing your partner.

3_Marriage is the chance to shape a new generation.

Not all couples want to have children and that's absolutely fine. But for those that do, marriage is an amazing way to bring children into a secure and stable environment. Couples tend to thrive in the challenge of teaching their children to become amazing individuals who will benefit society.

Child rearing can put strains on a marriage, but it can also make it stronger. After all, is there any challenge more fulfilling than raising children? Priorities change throughout marriages but ensuring that your partner is at the top of that list will enable you to overcome anything life throws at you.

4_Marriage means changing and growing as people.When you agree to share your life with somebody, you acknowledge that there will be bumps in the road that will change you along the way. By using most of these bumps and using them to enable you to grow together, your marriage will become stronger. You can enjoy the changing seasons of your marriage, holding hands through all of life's hurdles. The true meaning of marriage for many is that you grow together, and the marriage also grows and blossoms too.

Two

MEANING OF MARRIAGE TO THE AFRICANS

In African traditional societies, we know marriage as a sacred union between one man and one or more women excluding all others. This notion is extended to the union of two families, two communities or even two nations in the broader sense. With this union, comes certain well defined roles and responsibilities which has its foundation on communal sharing, respect and the promotion of obedience, selflessness, consideration. The fruits of this union which is always eagerly awaited by both families after the marriage are children. These children become the responsibility of both families to raise and guide. As they grow children have the responsibility to show their respect to these family members. As the extended family works together to raise the children, this put less strain on the mother who quickly regain her strength and energy to begin the birthing process again shortly after.

In the past, our mothers sole responsibility was to stay home, have children and care for them. This made them dependent and relied on their husbands for household or personal allowances, since even when she worked outside of the home, she generally engaged in petit trade or elementary teaching, with very limited income. As a result, this established a father figure dominance which tended to put our mothers in a submissive positions. Hence, she could not challenge his authority as doing this might put her in critical situations. (It is important to point out that in some traditional societies a man could decide to end a marriage and send the girl back to her parents for her disobedience or challenging his authority.) We must therefore note that women submissiveness was important because, it benefited not only her spouse but in some cases her family who needed their in-law's support to survive in some cases. Hence, as domestic partners, women main goal in marriage was to care for family and make her husband happy by bowing down to his demands amidst their frustrations. Our mothers accepted this role because that is all they knew. They modeled their marriage as that of their own parents and other relatives. This was the culture and it worked well for them at that time.

Today however, with modern changes in lifestyles in our African societies, comes new challenges. The advent of new technology, expansion in communication and increasing access to education opportunities, has made information available for everyone to process as they perceive it. Men and women begin to question things and seek other solutions for issues that would otherwise go unnoticed in the past. This has brought so much stress and challenges to traditional African families as we struggle between abiding to our old traditional values and adapting to the demands of modern societies. With more women becoming active participants in their homes; more women are getting a higher education which means better job opportunities and even the ability to earn more than their husbands; women having limited number of children which means more time to engage in other business opportunities; they are marrying latter which means have had time to get educated and massed their own wealth; and have found the freedom to express their needs which makes them more informed and demanding. Also, increasing migration and immigration, exposes families to new ways of lives and cultures which affects our abilities to strictly abide to our requirements to be domesticated partners. It therefore becomes pertinent to reevaluate the role and responsibilities of spouses in traditional African marriages to establish the balance needed for a contended and happy marriage. Time are changing and it is time to follow the signs of time.The notion of dominance and submissiveness worked well for our parents because families supported each other in marriage. Even when this didn't work, we cannot know since the culture reprimanded women from sharing personal marriage issues outside of immediate family. They could remain in marriage for fear of the unknown, for their children or inertia. Regardless of why they stayed, the longevity of their marriage cannot be interpreted as success as we don't know for sure what they endured and why they stayed. However, with massive migration from communal living in search of greener pastures, today's newly married couples are receiving lesser and lesser support from their immediate families, hence raising their children by themselves. This can be very stressful situation especially if one tries to dominate the other. Hence with so much responsibility endowed upon women in traditional African marriage, lack of spousal support leaves them overwhelmed with household chores especially since they both work long hours away from home. This often triggers disputes that may loom a crisis sparking the human desire to fightback to regain independence. For marriage to be successful therefore, each spouse must be willing to allow the other make their own choices rather than dominate. Doing so eliminates patterns of dominance and submissiveness which tends to destroy many homes. I believe the spouses must constantly remain in mutual agreement. Communication is ultimate as it enables the spouses to re-valuate their needs and make necessary adjustments for the proper functioning of their homes. Moreover, I have no problem being submissive to my husband, after all, he is the love of my life. However, my submissiveness must not be misinterpreted as a sign of weakness but rather an honor I choose to show my spouse.

In our marriage, we have well defined roles as husband and wife. As a modern-traditionalist woman, I have always found it my responsibility to care for my family and make sure that my home is kept clean, and children are cared for properly. But I also find it very attractive when my husband steps in to assist me with some household duties. As little as this help may be, it is very significant for my psychological wellbeing as it sends a positive message that I am not alone and someone care about me. Some little tasks as playing with the kids while I am cooking, sorting or doing the laundry, or even doing the dishes is not a lack of macho-ness, but rather augments the bond of love existing between spouses. This to me is the true meaning of complementing each other in marriage. It is being compassionate by seeing a need, and stepping in to fill it. It proves the oneness derived from your union in marriage. My spouse is amazing and his help has increased our bond of love and appreciation for each other as we teach our children the importance of teamwork to make the family happy. Above all we must not forget to crown this help with a restful parents' appreciation time as reward later in the day. This is ultimate to keep the bond of marriage even stronger.

The key ingredients to a healthy marriage is therefore are: love, honesty, respect, trust, communication and tolerance/understanding. We must not however confuse love and dependency since making time for intimacy in marriage solidifies the bond of oneness in marriage. I therefore encourage you my brothers and sisters who are getting ready to enter into this very beautiful sacred union to understand the changing times and adapt your needs with the times while sticking as much as possible to our values of mutual respect and honor which remains the core of African traditional marriage. Complement each other rather than dominate and/or attempt to put the other in a submissive position. Do not take each other for granted but rather acknowledge each other. Be happy, be yourself and enjoy your marriage which is a privilege from above.

Three

MEANING OF MARRIAGE TO THE WHITES

The whites gets married for companionship,to have a partner to share life experiences together,to have a backbone who will support them in their in life pursuits not like the blacks that destroys their career because of marriage,the whites get married to enjoy with their partners and not to come suffer unnecessary problems,they don't disturb themselves if no child comes but takes good care of the ones that comes their way be it a girl child or a boy child unlike the Africans who worry and kill themselves because of male children,the whites dislikes stress, the whites love a stress-free life unlike the blacks that worry over issues like childbirth ,male children and all the unnecessary problems that comes with marriage.

Four

ADVANTAGES OF MARRIAGE

Let's check out the advantages of married life and why to date marriage is the most wonderful relation apart from many other relationships that exist on this planet.

Merits and Advantages of Being Married

Companionship

Marriage can be seen as a true friendship between two people, who have either fallen in love or connected due to common interests and priorities.

We human beings cannot lead a solitary life and crave companionship. Life becomes more meaningful and joyful when we have someone to share our experiences, emotions, and concerns.

Trust

Marriage is an accepted way for two people to show their commitment and concern for each other. The best part is that apart from sharing your home, life, thoughts, secrets, distress you can blindly trust your partners like no other person on this planet except your parents or a true friend who cares for you.

Stability

Marriage is associated with stability and the admiration to give shape to your dreams via bringing up a family that includes your children, elders along with your spouse and experience the divinity of being a parent, a house maker or the bread earner of the family.

Financial Assistance

Often financial benefits are associated with marriage. You have someone to rely on and depend on to lead a happy and healthy life; especially when both the couple without are working and earnings for the welfare of the company.

On the other hand, if anyone of you is working and other is taking care of rest of the family chores including preparing a healthy diet for you, you find life a lot easier and can relish it without getting into too many stressful situations as you have someone to share responsibilities as well as workload.

Raising a Family

Marriage is about sharing your emotions, burdens, and responsibilities. Raising a child or looking after your parents or other elderly members of the family is relatively easier for two people than it is for one.

Reduces the risk of Sexually Transmitted Diseases

A happy married life promises and delivers a happy sex life. Partners can fulfill each others' desires in a trusting long-term relationship and reduce the health risks of sexually transmitted diseases.

Lifelong Motivation

A successful marriage and a supportive partner always motivate you to do better in life and keep growing a professional not only selfishly for yourself but your entire family including your parents, children and not to forget your spouse to whom your success matters equally!

Five

DISADVANTAGES OF MARRIAGE

You are viewed as little more than a source of income.

If you divorce, you'll be hit with alimony and child support payments for who knows how long.

You will pay for the house, car children and everything that goes with them (insurance utilities, gasoline, oil, etc.).

Your life revolves around the "abstract other". (Spouse, children, career). Your life is no longer your own!

If your wife decides to "monkey branch" to another man, Believe me, YOU'LL FOOT THE BILLS! If she decides to marry him, you'll pay for the children. (Why should HE adopt the children and wind up paying for them when YOU'RE his "meal ticket"?

You'll pay for everything! (Even your own funeral/burial).

You'll pay for Valentine's Day, vacations. everything!

If you divorce, you'll foot her attorney's fees as well as yours.

More includes

1. You are stuck with the same person forever

Some people believe that humans are not naturally monogamous. This is particularly true when we are younger. In fact, you could argue that it is more natural for us to sow our wild oats when we are young. So marriage in our youth is not ideal.

But what about marriage when we are older? Well, there are similar problems. As we age we might feel that life is passing us by and we are missing out on new experiences. We may be tempted by an affair and cheat on our partner.

2. It is expensive and a waste of money

Sure, you might save on your tax bill in the long run, but do you know how much the average wedding and honeymoon cost these days? In the UK it is around £32,000! I mean, who has that sort of money for one day and a week's holiday?

Of course, you could get married on a budget but people will notice and comment. With social media encouraging things like bride-shaming and wedding cake shaming, do you really want to take the risk of putting on a cheapie wedding?

3. Half of the marriages end in divorce anyway

Did you know that only a few years ago nearly 50% of all marriages in the US ended in divorce? This rate is dropping thanks to millennials who are marrying and staying married.

But you might wonder to yourself 'What is the point' when so many marriages fail? Why spend all that money in the first place on something that doesn't have much chance of working out?

4. Marriage is bad for women's health

Overall marriage is good for your health, however, not so much if you are a woman. In the US, 55% of women wanted to end their marriage compared to just 29% of men. But why do women feel unhappy once they tie the knot?

Men still traditionally earn more than women so they tend to wield more power in the relationship. Women also do more of the childcare and give up their careers to look after children. As a result, they are reliant on their husbands for money. This leaves them powerless and vulnerable.

Even women who don't have children and do have careers still end up doing the majority of the household chores. Men will spend their leisure time on hobbies and catching up with friends. On the other hand, women will tidy the house, do the washing, and fix the meals. If she asks hubby for help she's nagging him.

5. Marriage traps you

It's all well and good if you are happy and in a great relationship, but what about abusive marriages? Domestic violence and coercive control are common in all kinds of situations. However, once you are married it is much more difficult to extract yourself from your spouse.

Couples may argue about property or custody issues with the children. Your spouse might oppose the divorce and this can cost money going through solicitors and the courts. And what about the children's welfare? You might also stay in a bad marriage simply because you are married.

6. It's old fashioned

Despite many young people getting hitched, marriage is seen to many as a traditional institution. Some even view it as a way of conforming to societal norms. Then there are others that think marriage should be available to everyone, including same-sex couples.

On the other hand, you may argue why should you get married to show your love to your partner? There are lots of kinds of relationships these days that don't have a certificate to prove their love. Marriage isn't the only option for people these days.

7. You like being financially independent

I wouldn't like to have a joint bank account with anyone! Even if that person was my husband. I have always taken care of my own finances and I don't intend to give over half of my stuff to someone else just because of a bit of paper.

That might sound pretty unromantic but when you've worked hard all your life and when you are a woman you have to be careful. Then again, before you start judging me, I wouldn't expect a future husband to hand me half his stuff either!

8. It is more expensive to be married

Just as there are financial reasons to marry, so are financial reasons not to. It is correct to think that as a married couple you will be entitled to certain tax breaks but be warned. There are also marriage tax penalties.

It all depends on how much you both earn. You may find that if you both make a similar amount of money you could risk a penalty. Couples tend to get the tax break when one earns significantly less than the other.

9. Blended families

For those marrying when they are older there's a chance that they will have children from a previous relationship. It's also possible that you have your own kids to think about as well. Not to mention in-laws, uncles and aunts and grandparents.

Your partner may have financial obligations to his former spouse and you may also lose some benefits should you enter into a new marriage. Then there's the problem of everyone getting along. If the children do not like the new partner this can put friction on the marriage.

Six

MARRIAGE A DIE OR DO THING?

Marriage is not a do-or-die affair or a guarantee of happiness or a secured future. Singleness also has its own benefits while it lasts, but some ladies would rather stay in an abusive relationship or courtship just because they believe they are running out of time and that age is no longer on their side. Ladies approaching their late 20s and clocking 30 or even 40, think that it should not be heard that they do not have a boyfriend or suitor.

It is better to be single and have your life in sound health and be happy, than being in a relationship that saps your emotional, financial and physical energy, leaving you almost useless.

There are surely benefits that come from being patient and remaining single until the right person comes, and also leaving your life the right way. These include the opportunity to engage in developmental activities, such as further studies, volunteering in social activities that are beneficial to other people; Freedom from heartache and emotional trauma that comes from an abusive relationship where marriage is not guaranteed; opportunity to remain emotionally settled and balanced and enjoying your singleness doing the right things while it lasts; opportunity to develop yourself both emotionally and psychologically in order to be prepared for Mr or Miss Right; and opportunity to enjoy other good things that come with being single.

Crossing age 30 without a spouse is not the end of the world. And for those who are good with extracting the blessing out of every disappointment, it may well be the actual beginning of life!

Seven

MUST YOU MARRY?

Marriage is a powerful creator and sustainer of human and social capital for adults as well as children, about as important as education when it comes to promoting the health, wealth, and well-being of adults and communities.

questions: "Is marriage a dying institution? And do we still need it?"

Why get married?

A young man at a marriage conference where Erin and I were speaking once asked me, "Why get married? I love my girlfriend and I'm committed to her. I do all of the things that you're encouraging us to do to have a strong and healthy relationship. Why do we need a couple of expensive rings and a piece of paper to prove our love?"

It's a good question. And to answer it, we need to start with the apostle Paul.

When Paul wrote to the Ephesians, he had a lot to say about marriage. " 'Therefore a man shall leave his father and mother and hold fast to his wife, and the two shall become one flesh.' This mystery is profound," he wrote in Ephesians 5:31-32.

And he's right. The commitment we make when we enter into a marriage — when we become "one flesh"— is indeed profound and mysterious.

In God's eyes, marriage is much more than a formal declaration of love and commitment between two people. Here are nine reasons to get married, although there are undoubtedly others:

1. Marriage is the cornerstone of a stable society

Why do great civilizations collapse? What happened to Carthage, Egypt, Greece, Rome and other ancient superpowers? While there are many reasons for the decline and fall of an empire, historians have identified the breakdown of the family as a main contributing factor.

"History shows that the strength of any nation depends upon the strength of its families," writes Gerald Flurry in The Trumpet. "Family is the rock-solid foundation on which a country's superstructure is erected."

Families provide built-in support systems, financial security and health benefits for people. They ensure children are educated and communities thrive.

"The family is the first and vital cell of society," Pope John Paul II once said. "As the family goes, so goes the nation, and so goes the whole world in which we live."

Those families begin with a husband and wife, and their union welds society together. Creating a stronger world for your kids to live in is a pretty good reason to get married.

2. Marriage is a sacred covenant between the couple and God

During a traditional wedding ceremony, the man and woman make this vow: "I take you to be my wedded wife/husband, and I do promise and covenant, before God and these witnesses, to be your loving and faithful husband/wife, to have and to hold from this day forward, for better, for worse, for richer, for poorer, in sickness and in health, to love and to cherish, until we are parted by death."

When you get married, you're making a lifelong promise to God and each other. You don't do this if you're cohabitating. In our culture, I'm not sure if young couples really understand the seriousness of the wedding vow. But God certainly does. Take a look at Matthew 19:4-6:

He answered, "Have you not read that he who created them from the beginning made them male and female, and said, 'Therefore a man shall leave his father and his mother and hold fast to his wife, and the two shall become one flesh'? So they are no longer two but one flesh. What therefore God has joined together, let not man separate" (emphasis added).

God is involved in a marriage, which is what makes it a sacred agreement that's supposed to last a lifetime. This is just one of the reasons marriage and living together are vastly different.

marriage, which is what makes it a sacred agreement that's supposed to last a lifetime. This is just one of the reasons marriage and living together are vastly different.

3. Marriage benefits the individuals

Compared to singles, married people tend to be happier, healthier, safer and wealthier. They enjoy certain tax deductions, have better health insurance coverage and statistically have the most satisfying sex on the planet!

According to federal law, there are 1,138 benefits, rights and protections provided on the basis of marital status. As romantic as a good tax break sounds, these advantages would never inspire someone to get down on bended knee and beseech their beloved to spend a lifetime together. I didn't ask Erin to marry me for better insurance coverage.

But I did know that the marriage would benefit me. I wanted to experience life with my best friend. I wanted to enjoy passion and laughter, deep connection and shared dreams and, most importantly,

I wanted to pursue Christ with Erin. The anticipation of experiencing these and many other wonderful things for the rest of our lives is why I married my wife. Who wouldn't want that?

4. Marriage is the best way to raise children

Married parents tend to provide a safer and healthier home environment for their kids. On average, children in these families:

Fare better in school.

Exhibit fewer behavioral problems.

Are more likely to form healthy romantic relationships as adults.

And did you know that the way your kids see you treat your spouse is how they will treat their own spouse someday? A son learns how to be a husband and how women should treat him by seeing how his parents interact. A daughter learns how to be a wife and how men should treat her by watching her parents. So if you love and respect each other, your children will want to do the same in their marriage. Your marriage is your child's blueprint for intimacy and relationships.

5. Marriage creates a safe relationship where you can reach the deepest levels of intimacy and connection

When two people make a lifelong commitment before God and to each other, they create a level of safety and security that can't be replicated in any other human relationship.

When spouses truly trust the vows they made on their wedding day, they're willing to be naked and unashamed, just as Adam and Eve were in the Garden of Eden (Genesis 2:25). They can be completely known by their spouse at the deepest levels: spiritually, emotionally, mentally and physically. They experience a profound vulnerability and openness that can't happen in other relationships.

I'm not suggesting that every married couple actually reaches this level of intimacy, but the potential is there — and it's unique to marriage. How's that for a reason to get married?

6. Marriage creates a powerful synergy

The Oxford Dictionary defines synergy as "the cooperation of two or more elements to produce a combined effect greater than the sum of their separate effects." You could almost define marriage the same way.

Let me repeat what Paul wrote in Ephesians: "The two shall become one flesh. This is mystery is profound …" The profound mystery is how a man and woman, even with all of their differences, can be united as one in marriage.

This "oneness" is a superpower. When a husband and wife are unified, they can accomplish amazing feats together. When they're united in vision and pursue a shared dream together, they can serve God in powerful ways.

Pastor Francis Chan said, "Picture marriage as a vehicle for mission, an opportunity for Christians to carry out our mission to make disciples of all the nations."

God wants you to use your superpower, your oneness, to bless others and do extraordinary things for the Kingdom of God. He doesn't want you to hoard the power He's given you. Your marriage should be about something bigger than individual gratification, petty arguments and the pursuit of pleasure. Inwardly focused marriages are not fulfilling. Find a vision for your marriage that you both are passionate about and use your synergy to benefit others.

7. Marriage helps us become more like Christ

Is marriage designed to make us "happy" or "holy"? Actually, it makes us both. God created marriage to be much more than a relationship that meets our needs and gives us happiness.

That's why holiness always outweighs happiness. In fact, God's preeminent goal for your marriage is not your mutual happiness at all — it's Christlikeness. As Paul explained, "For those whom he foreknew he also predestined to be conformed to the image of his Son …" (Romans 8:29; emphasis added).

Now, you'll surely find happiness if you cooperate with God's purpose for your marriage. But He wants so much more than happiness for you; He wants joy. He wants impact. He wants your marriage to have significance and spiritual power and a compelling attractiveness that turns people's heads. God designed marriage — with its joys and its trials, its ups and its downs, its good times and its bad times — to help you to grow to be more like Christ.

This process isn't easy. It's not supposed to be. But once you understand that fact, marriage's inevitable conflicts and rough times don't feel quite so threatening. This seems so simple; a great marriage is the outcome of becoming Christlike.

That said, to suggest that marriage is only designed to bring spiritual growth through fiery trial is a complete misreading of God's intent. If marriage points to the final wedding of Christ and His Church, then there must be a sense in which it's designed to bring joy and bliss. Just as parents delight in seeing their children happy and thriving, our heavenly Father desires to see us happy and thriving in our marriages.

8. Marriage gives us the help we need

Genesis 2:18 says, "The LORD God said, 'It is not good that man should be alone; I will make him a helper fit for him.' ". Our spouses can give us help that the world doesn't offer. Having lifelong help from the human being who knows us best is a great reason to choose marriage.

Just to be clear, the Bible makes a big distinction between what we should deal with ourselves and when we should seek help. Galatians 6:5 says, "for each will have to bear his own load." The Greek word for load means "cargo," a light problem that individuals must carry. Think of it as a backpack.

But just a few verses earlier in Galatians 6:2, we're told to "Bear one another's burdens." The Greek word for burden means something that's heavy, something that's too much for one person to bear alone. Instead of a backpack, it's more like a huge steamer trunk on our shoulders.

Paul is saying that we shouldn't allow a person to be crushed under the excessive weight of their burdens.

these burdens for each other. To help carry them, we must be there when needed.

9. Marriage reflects the relationship between Christ and the Church, and the healthy family is our greatest witness to a lost world

Marriage points to the final marriage of Christ, the Bridegroom, with His bride, the church (Revelation 19-21).

A healthy marriage also provides a strong evangelism opportunity. In his book Life-Style Evangelism, Joe Aldrich writes:

The two greatest forces in evangelism are a healthy church and a healthy marriage. The two are interdependent. You can't have one without the other. It is the healthy marriage, however, that is the true 'frontline weapon.' The Christian family in a community is the ultimate evangelistic tool, assuming the home circle is an open one in which the beauty of the gospel is readily available. It's the old story: When love is seen, the message is heard, or to put it more succinctly… more is caught than taught.

The marriages of Christian couples who have allowed the Lord to redeem and bless them personally and relationally become a living testimony to the Lord. Their stories bless other couples and benefit the Kingdom of God.

Choose God's best

Wonder. Joy. Intimacy. Purpose. If those qualities matter to you, then don't be afraid of marriage. A marriage that's consistent with God's design will allow you to experience all of those things together.

At Focus on the Family, we believe there are many reasons to get married and not just cohabitate. We believe that God's design for marriage is a lifelong covenant where a husband and wife are relentlessly growing as individuals into the image of Christ and creating a relationship that both people are thrilled with.

Remember that man who wondered, "Why get married?" As this young man and I talked during each session break, I unpacked the reasons marriage matters. At the end of the conference, the man told me that he wanted to honor God and provide the very best for his girlfriend.

"I'm taking her ring shopping," he said.

Months later, I received a wedding invitation.

I know the young man and his new bride will have plenty of challenges ahead of them. Anyone who marries always does. But are those challenges worth it? You bet they are. Because marriage matters, and there are more than enough reasons to make that commitment.

Seven Reasons Not to Marry

The decision to marry is the biggest decision that most people make in a lifetime. Following is a list of danger signs. If any of these are present in your relationship now, it is best to postpone the marriage until the issue is resolved. Marriage itself will not make these problems disappear. In fact, these problems almost always get worse after marriage.

1. Marrying to get out of the house.

This is simply trading one set of problems for another. Other options exist to get away from a troubled home. A counselor can help you find them.

2. No one better will ask me to marry him/her.

This kind of thinking suggests that you don't think much of yourself. People who think this way aren't sure enough of themselves to hold their own in marriage and are generally unhappy when they do find their true selves. Postponing or canceling your wedding is a good idea. Some good counseling can help, too.

3. It's just time to get married.

Actually, what is needed is the right time AND the right person.

4. Being hit, slapped, threatened or intimidated, verbally put down, or forced to do things you don't want to do by your partner.

Being treated like this is wrong and you should not put up with it. This is not the normal way that engaged or married couples relate to one another. Marriage is based on respect, not fear and force. Don't be fooled by your partner's promise to stop.

5. You or your partner are dependent on drugs and/or alcohol. Some of the symptoms of dependence include:

One of you uses drugs or alcohol to escape from problems or worries.

Getting drugs or alcohol is always on your mind.

You can't have fun or relax without drugs or alcohol.

You become careless with important relationships.

You drink alone or in secret.

A person dependent on drugs and alcohol is not a free person. Their love affair is with the bottle or drugs – not with you!

6. You and your partner have major items which you avoid talking about because it might upset your relationship.

For example: children, money management, division of responsibility for home and children, whether to keep both careers, religious identity of children in an interfaith marriage.

You need to talk about all important issues openly before marriage. The wedding ceremony itself will not eliminate the issues or the effects of your disagreements. Consider enlisting the help of a priest, minister, or counselor if these issues seem too threatening to handle alone.

So MUST YOU MARRY?

_YES if u are ready for it,if you are prepared,if you can cope and if it is something you can handle.

_NO if u can't handle it,if you can't submit and subject yourself to your husband and give your children quality time,if you are ready to sacrifice it all,being married doesn't make you the best and being single doesn't make you the worst,just do what makes you happy and live your life to the fullest.

www.ingramcontent.com/pod-product-compliance
Lightning Source LLC
LaVergne TN
LVHW020530160826
845677LV00015B/3993

* 9 7 9 8 3 5 2 7 1 2 0 4 7 *